WINGS

Written by

JANE YOLEN

Illustrated by

DENNIS NOLAN

Harcourt Brace Jovanovich, Publishers

SAN DIEGO NEW YORK LONDON

A B O U T   T H E   S T O R Y

An architect, sculptor, and inventor, Daedalus was revered by the artist guilds of Greece. Buildings that once stood in Sardinia, Egypt, and Italy were attributed to him as well as a famous statue of Heracles in Thebes.

Well thought of in Athens, where he was a prince, Daedalus lost all popular support when he impulsively killed his nephew, Talos, who seemed destined to pass him in skill.

Exiled to Crete, Daedalus was credited with building the famed labyrinth. Later he was imprisoned, either for high treason or because the king feared he would reveal the secret of the maze.

The sea in which Icarus is said to have drowned now bears his name — the Icarian Sea. In some versions of the legend his body is found by his father. In others he is washed ashore and discovered by Heracles, who buries him on an island thereafter called Icaria. In yet other versions his body is never recovered.

The story of Daedalus and Icarus has inspired many writers. Homer mentions Daedalus in *The Iliad*. The Roman poet Ovid and the Greek playwright Apollodorus both wrote full versions of the tale. Ovid's retelling in *Metamorphoses* is in poetic form. In each version it is the Greek passion for punishing *hubris* — pride — that remains at the core of the tale. In this telling, the judgment of that pride is spoken as if by a Greek chorus.

Library of Congress Cataloging-in-Publication Data
Yolen, Jane.
Wings/by Jane Yolen; illustrated by Dennis Nolan. — 1st ed.
p.   cm.
Summary: The story of Daedalus, the Greek master craftsman, who murdered his nephew because of envy, fled to Crete, and then, with his son, tried to fly away from Crete like a bird.
ISBN 0-15-297850-X
1. Daedalus (Greek mythology) — Juvenile literature.
[1. Daedalus (Greek mythology) 2. Mythology, Greek.]
I. Nolan, Dennis, ill.   II. Title.
BL820.D25Y64   1991
398.22′0938 — dc20   90-4886

The illustrations in this book were done in Winsor & Newton watercolors on Arches watercolor paper.
The display type was set in Bauer Text Initials.
The text type was set in Meridien.
Composition by Thompson Type, San Diego, California
Color separations were made by Bright Arts, Ltd., Singapore.
Printed by Holyoke Lithograph, Springfield, Massachusetts
Bound by Horowitz/Rae Book Manufacturers, Inc., Fairfield, New Jersey
Production supervision by Warren Wallerstein and Michele Green
Designed by Michael Farmer

Printed in the United States of America

B C D E

For my dear friends at HBJ
— J. Y.

For Pythagoras, Professor Appleton, and the Golden Ratio
— D. N.

ONCE IN ANCIENT GREECE, when the gods dwelt on a high mountain overseeing the world, there lived a man named Daedalus who was known for the things he made.

He invented the axe, the bevel, and the awl. He built statues that were so lifelike they seemed ready to move. He designed a maze whose winding passages opened one into another as if without beginning, as if without end.

But Daedalus never understood the labyrinth of his own heart. He was clever but he was not always kind. He was full of pride but he did not give others praise. He was a maker — but he was a taker, too.

The gods always punish such a man.

Athens was the queen of cities and she had her princes. Daedalus was one. He was a prince and he was an artist, and he was proud of being both.

The very elements were his friends, and the people of Athens praised him.

"The gods will love you forever, Daedalus," they cried out to him as he walked through the city streets.

The gods listened and did not like to be told what to do.

A man who hears only praise becomes deaf. A man who sees no rival to his art becomes blind. Though he grew rich and he grew famous in the city, Daedalus also grew lazy and careless. And one day, without thought for the consequences, he caused the death of his young nephew, Prince Talos, who fell from a tall temple.

Even a prince cannot kill a prince. The king of Athens punished Daedalus by sending him away, away from all he loved: away from the colorful pillars of the temples, away from the noisy, winding streets, away from the bustling shops and stalls, away from his smithy, away from the sound of the dark sea. He would never be allowed to return.

And the gods watched the exile from on high.

Many days and nights Daedalus fled from his past. He crossed strange lands. He crossed strange seas. All he carried with him was a goatskin flask, the clothes on his back, and the knowledge in his hands. All he carried with him was grief that he had caused a child's death and grief that Athens was now dead to him.

He traveled a year and a day until he came at last to the island of Crete, where the powerful King Minos ruled.

The sands of Crete were different from his beloved Athens, the trees in the meadow were different, the flowers and the houses and the little, dark-eyed people were different. Only the birds seemed the same to Daedalus, and the sky — the vast, open, empty road of the sky.

But the gods found nothing below them strange.

Daedalus knew nothing of Crete but Crete knew much of Daedalus, for his reputation had flown on wings before him. King Minos did not care that Daedalus was an exile or that he had been judged guilty of a terrible crime.

"You are the world's greatest builder, Daedalus," King Minos said. "Build me a labyrinth in which to hide a beast."

"A cage would be simpler," said Daedalus.

"This is no ordinary beast," said the king. "This is a monster. This is a prince. His name is Minotaur and he is my wife's own son. He has a bull's head but a man's body. He eats human flesh. I cannot kill the queen's child. Even a king cannot kill a prince. And I cannot put him in a cage. But in a maze such as you might build, I could keep him hidden forever."

Daedalus bowed his head, but he smiled at the king's praise. He built a labyrinth for the king with countless corridors and winding ways. He devised such cunning passages that only he knew the secret pathway to its heart—he, and the Minotaur who lived there.

Yet the gods marked the secret way as well.

For many years Daedalus lived on the island of Crete, delighting in the praise he received from king and court. He made hundreds of new things for them. He made dolls with moving parts and a dancing floor inlaid with wood and stone for the princess Ariadne. He made iron gates for the king and queen wrought with cunning designs. He grew fond of the little dark-eyed islanders, and he married a Cretan wife. A son was born to them whom Daedalus named Icarus. The boy was small like his mother but he had his father's quick, bright ways.

Daedalus taught Icarus many things, yet the one Daedalus valued most was the language of his lost Athens. Though he had a grand house and servants to do his bidding, though he had a wife he loved and a son he adored, Daedalus was not entirely happy. His heart still lay in Athens, the land of his youth, and the words he spoke with his son helped keep the memory of Athens alive.

One night a handsome young man came to Daedalus' house, led by a lovesick Princess Ariadne. The young man spoke with Daedalus in that Athenian tongue.

"I am Theseus, a prince of Athens, where your name is still remembered with praise. It is said that Daedalus was more than a prince, that he had the gods in his hands. Surely such a man has not forgotten Athens."

Daedalus shook his head. "I thought Athens had forgotten me."

"Athens remembers and Athens needs your help, O prince," said Theseus.

"Help? What help can I give Athens, when I am so far from home?"

"Then you do not know . . . ," Theseus began.

"Know what?"

"That every seven years Athens must send a tribute of boys and girls to King Minos. He puts them into the labyrinth you devised and the monster Minotaur devours them there."

Horrified, Daedalus thought of the bright-eyed boys and girls he had known in Athens. He thought of his own dark-eyed son asleep in his cot. He remembered his nephew, Talos, whose eyes had been closed by death. "How can I help?"

"Only you know the way through the maze," said Theseus. "Show me the way that I may slay the monster."

"I will show you," said Daedalus thoughtfully, "but Princess Ariadne must go as well. The Minotaur is her half-brother. He will not hurt her. She will be able to lead you to him, right into the heart of the maze."

The gods listened to the plan and nodded gravely.

Daedalus drew them a map and gave Princess Ariadne a thread to tie at her waist, that she might unwind it as they went and so find the way back out of the twisting corridors.

Hand in hand, Theseus and Ariadne left and Daedalus went into his son's room. He looked down at the sleeping boy.

"I am a prince of Athens," he whispered. "I did what must be done."

If Icarus heard his father's voice, he did not stir. He was dreaming still as Ariadne and Theseus threaded their way to the very center of the maze. And before he awakened, they had killed the Minotaur and fled from Crete, taking the boys and girls of Athens with them. They took all hope of Daedalus' safety as well.

Then the gods looked thoughtful and they did not smile.

When King Minos heard that the Minotaur had been slain and Ariadne taken, he guessed that Daedalus had betrayed him, for no one else knew the secret of the maze. He ordered Daedalus thrown into a high prison tower.

"Thus do kings reward traitors!" cried Minos. Then he added, "See that you care for your own son better than you cared for my wife's unfortunate child." He threw Icarus into the tower, too, and slammed the great iron gate shut with his own hand.

The tiny tower room, with its single window overlooking the sea, was Daedalus' home now. Gone was Athens where he had been a prince, gone was Crete where he had been a rich man. All he had left was one small room, with a wooden bench and straw pallets on the floor.

Day after day young Icarus stood on the bench and watched through the window as the seabirds dipped and soared over the waves.

"Father!" Icarus called each day. "Come and watch the birds."

But Daedalus would not. Day after day, he leaned against the wall or lay on a pallet bemoaning his fate and cursing the gods who had done this thing to him.

The gods heard his curses and they grew angry.

One bright day Icarus took his father by the hand, leading him to the window.

"Look, Father," he said, pointing to the birds. "See how beautiful their wings are. See how easily they fly."

Just to please the boy, Daedalus looked. Then he clapped his hands to his eyes. "What a fool I have been," he whispered. "What a fool. Minos may have forbidden me sea and land, but he has left me the air. Oh, my son, though the king is ever so great and powerful, he does not rule the sky. It is the gods' own road and I am a favorite of the gods. To think a child has shown me the way!"

Every day after that, Daedalus and Icarus coaxed the birds to their windows with bread crumbs saved from their meager meals. And every day gulls, gannets, and petrels, cormorants and pelicans, shearwaters and grebes, came to the sill. Daedalus stroked the feeding birds with his clever hands and harvested handfuls of feathers. And Icarus, as if playing a game, grouped the feathers on the floor in order of size, just as his father instructed.

But it was no game. Soon the small piles of feathers became big piles, the big piles, great heaps. Then clever Daedalus, using a needle he had shaped from a bit of bone left over from dinner and thread pulled out of his own shirt, sewed together small feathers, overlapping them with the larger, gently curving them in great arcs. He fastened the ends with molded candle wax and made straps with the leather from their sandals.

At last Icarus understood. "Wings, Father!" he cried, clapping his hands together in delight. "Wings!"

At that the gods laughed, and it was thunder over water.

They made four wings in all, a pair for each of them. Icarus had the smaller pair, for he was still a boy. They practiced for days in the tower, slipping their arms through the straps, raising and lowering the wings, until their arms had grown strong and used to the weight. They hid the wings beneath their pallets whenever the guards came by.

At last they were ready. Daedalus kneeled before his son.

"Your arms are strong now, Icarus," he said, "but do not forget my warning."

The boy nodded solemnly, his dark eyes wide. "I must not fly too low or the water will soak the feathers. I must not fly too high or the sun will melt the wax."

"Remember," his father said. "Remember."

The gods trembled, causing birds to fall through the bright air.

Daedalus climbed onto the sill. The wings made him clumsy but he did not fall. He helped Icarus up.

First the child, then the man, leaped out into the air. They pumped once and then twice with their arms. The wind caught the feathers of the wings and pushed them upward into the Cretan sky.

Wingtip to wingtip they flew, writing the lines of their escape on the air. Some watchers below took them for eagles. Most took them for gods.

As they flew, Daedalus concentrated on long, steady strokes. He remembered earlier days, when the elements had been his friends: fire and water and air. Now, it seemed, they were his friends once more.

But young Icarus had no such memories to steady his wings. He beat them with abandon, glorying in his freedom. He slipped away from his father's careful pattern along a wild stream of wind.

"Icarus, my son — remember!" Daedalus cried out.

But Icarus spiraled higher and higher and higher still. He did not hear his father's voice. He heard only the music of the wind; he heard only the sighing of the gods.

He passed the birds. He passed the clouds. He passed into the realm of the sun. Too late he felt the wax run down his arms; too late he smelled the singe of feathers. Surprised, he hung solid in the air. Then, like a star in nova, he tumbled from the sky, down, down, down into the waiting sea.

And the gods wept bitterly for the child.

"Where are you, my son?" Daedalus called. He circled the water, looking desperately for some sign. All he saw were seven feathers afloat on the sea, spinning into different patterns with each passing wave.

Weeping, he flew away over the dark sea to the isle of Sicily. There he built a temple to the god Apollo, for Apollo stood for life and light and never grew old but remained a beautiful boy forever. On the temple walls Daedalus hung up his beautiful wings as an offering to the bitter wisdom of the gods.

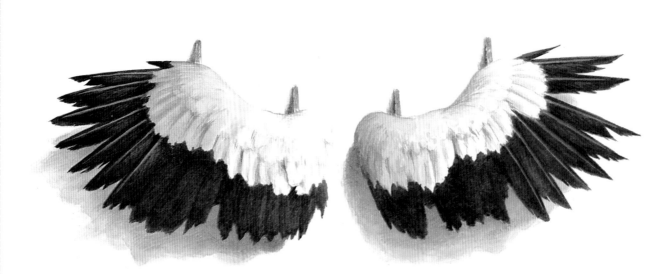

So Daedalus' story ended — and yet it did not. For in Sicily he was received kindly by King Cocalus, who was well pleased with his skills.

Meanwhile, back in Crete, enraged at his prisoners' escape, King Minos was determined to find and punish them. He proclaimed a great reward for anyone skilled enough to pass a silken thread through the closed spiral of a seashell. He knew that if Daedalus was alive, he could not resist the lure of such a game.

Daedalus was sure he could easily solve the puzzle. He bored a small hole in one end of a shell, moistened it with a bit of honey, then closed up the hole. Fastening a thread to an ant, he put the insect into the shell. The ant scurried through the twisting labyrinth toward the sweet smell, running as easily as Princess Ariadne had run through the maze with the thread unwinding at her waist. When the ant emerged from the other end, it had pulled the silken thread through the spirals of the shell.

Though he used a false name to claim the prize, Daedalus did not fool King Minos. Minos knew the winner was his old enemy. So, with a mighty army, Minos sailed to Sicily to bring Daedalus back.

But King Cocalus would not give up Daedalus to the foreign invaders, and a great battle was fought. With Daedalus' help, King Cocalus was victorious and King Minos was killed. Minos was clever but he was not kind. He had a heart scabbed over with old remembered wounds.

The gods always punish such a man.